ANCIENT EGYPT

PHARAOHS & PRIESTS

Jane Shuter

Heinemann Library
Des Plaines, Illinois

Designed by Clare Sleven
Illustrations by Jonathan Adams, Jeff Edwards
Printed in Hong Kong

03 02 01 00 99
10 9 8 7 6 5 4 3 2 1

Library of Congress Cataloging-in-Publication Data

Shuter, Jane.
        Pharoahs and priests / Jane Shuter.
            p.   cm. -- (Ancient Egypt)
        Includes bibliographical references (p.) and index.
        Summary: Discusses the role of pharoahs, priests, gods, goddesses, and various other official figures in ancient Egyptian society, and explains the rituals practiced when death occurred.
        ISBN 1-57572-731-5 (lib. bdg.)
        1. Pharoahs--Juvenile literature. 2. Priests--Egypt--Juvenile literature. 3. Egypt--Officials and employees--Juvenile literature. 4. Egypt--Religion--Juvenile literature. [1. Egypt--Civilization--To 332 B.C. 2. Egypt--Antiquities. 3. Funeral rites and ceremonies--Egypt.] I. Title. II. Series: Shuter, Jane. Ancient Egypt.
        DT61.S645   1998
        932--dc21   98-9471
                                                                             CIP
                                                                             AC

Acknowledgements
The Publishers would like to thank the following for permission to reproduce photographs: Ancient Art & Architecture Collection: J. Stevens p. 9; British Museum: pp. 7, 13, 17; Hildesheim Museum: p. 22; Michael Holford: p. 14; Photo Archive: J. Liepe pp. 5, 27; Roger Scruton: pp.15, 23; Werner Forman Archive: p. 11.

Cover photograph reproduced with permission of John Stevens, Ancient Art & Architecture Collection

Every effort has been made to contact copyright holders of any material reproduced in this book. Any omissions will be rectified in subsequent printings if notice is given to the Publisher.

Any words appearing in the text in bold, **like this**, are explained in the Glossary.

CONTENTS

Introduction   4

Gods and Goddesses   6

The Pharaoh   8

Mayor and Chief Priest   10

Priests   12

Wabs   14

Priestesses   16

Temples   18

Dealing with the Dead   20

Mummies: How Do We Know?   22

Tombs   24

Egypt and Other Lands   26

How Do We Know How Egypt
   Was Organized?   28

Glossary   30

More Books to Read   32

Index   32

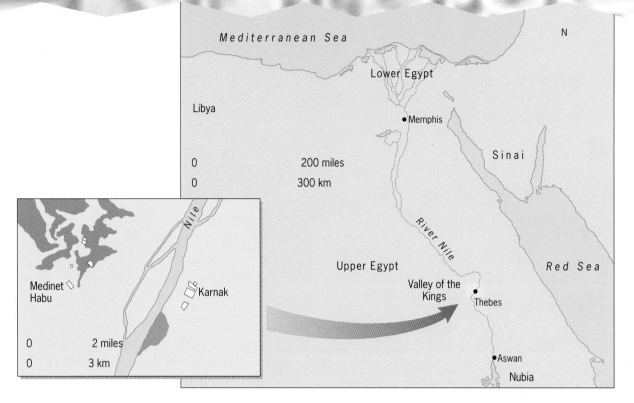

Medinet Habu

Karnak

Nile

0   2 miles
0   3 km

Mediterranean Sea

Lower Egypt

Libya

• Memphis

0   200 miles
0   300 km

Sinai

Upper Egypt

River Nile

Valley of the Kings

• Thebes

Red Sea

• Aswan

Nubia

N

This chart shows different times in the long history of Ancient Egypt. The red blocks show when pharaohs were weak and no one ran the whole country.

Ancient Egypt's history began in about 3000 B.C., when two kingdoms, Upper and Lower Egypt, were joined together and ruled by one **pharaoh** (king) named Narmer.

PHARAOHS

The pharaoh had all the power and owned all the land. Many pharaohs were worshiped as gods. People thought they made the sun rise and the **crops** grow.

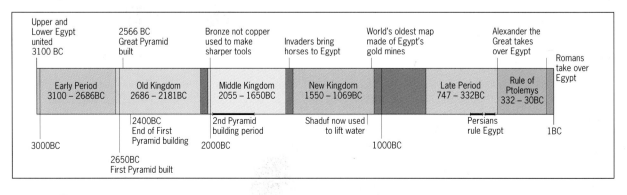

Upper and Lower Egypt united 3100 BC

2566 BC Great Pyramid built

Bronze not copper used to make sharper tools

Invaders bring horses to Egypt

World's oldest map made of Egypt's gold mines

Alexander the Great takes over Egypt

Romans take over Egypt

| Early Period 3100 – 2686BC | Old Kingdom 2686 – 2181BC | Middle Kingdom 2055 – 1650BC | New Kingdom 1550 – 1069BC | | Late Period 747 – 332BC | Rule of Ptolemys 332 – 30BC |

2400BC End of First Pyramid building

2nd Pyramid building period

Shaduf now used to lift water

Persians rule Egypt

3000BC

2650BC First Pyramid built

2000BC

1000BC

1BC

EVERYONE ELSE

The pharaoh was in charge. But **officials** ran Egypt for him. Some of them controlled huge areas of the country. They had a great deal of power. Other officials had less important jobs. Many officials also worked as **priests** for three months of the year and organized the **temples**. Ordinary people had no say in how the country was run or how gods and goddesses were worshiped. They just did as they were told.

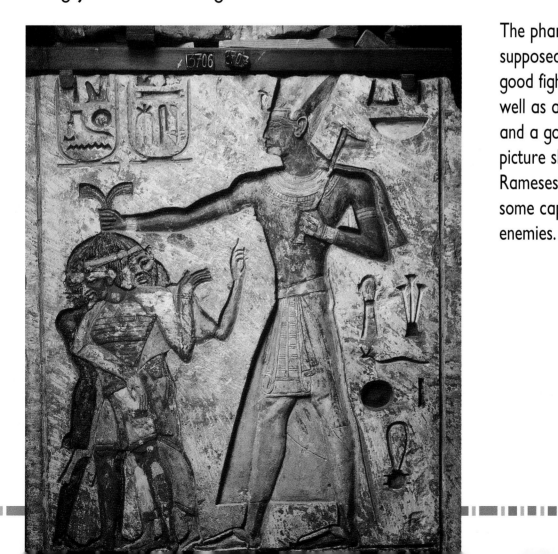

The pharaoh was supposed to be a good fighter as well as a ruler and a god. This picture shows Rameses II with some captured enemies.

The Egyptians believed in many gods and goddesses. They also believed that any one of the gods could affect their lives at any time. So all the gods had to be kept happy. In paintings, the gods were often given the head of an animal and the body of a person.

WHO DID WHAT?

Gods and goddesses controlled different things. Some gods and goddesses were worshiped by all Egyptians, like Hathor, goddess of the sky, and Amun, god of the sun. Some gods were only worshiped in some parts of Egypt, like Sobek the crocodile-headed god. Some gods were "household gods." They were worshiped at **shrines** in the home. They ran things in everyday life, like health or childbirth.

MAGIC

The Egyptians believed in magic as well as prayers to the gods. They carried **amulets** to help keep themselves safe. Doctors said spells when they gave patients medicine.

The bird-headed god, Thoth, writes down the answer.

Ani's ba, the link between his body and his spirit, sits on a shrine waiting for the answer.

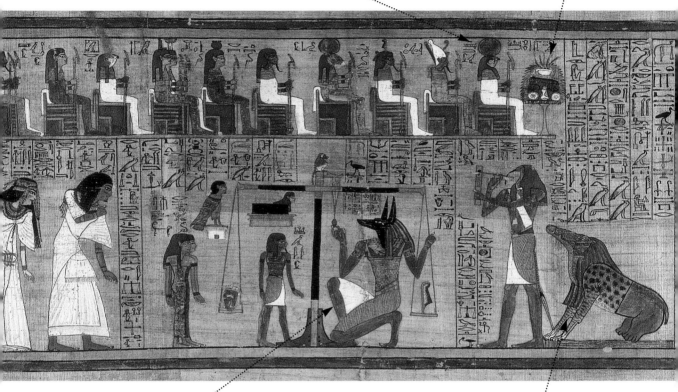

The jackal-headed god, Anubis, weighs Ani's heart (in the jar on the left balance) against the Feather of Truth to see if Ani has lived a good life.

If Ani has lived a bad life, then Ammut, the animal with the head of a crocodile, the chest of a lion, and the back of a hippo, will eat him.

In this picture, the gods and goddesses judge the **scribe** Ani (on the left) to see if he led a good life. The picture comes from a book buried with Ani in about 1250 B.C.

The **pharaoh** ruled all of Ancient Egypt. He was also the most important religious leader—the link between the gods and the Egyptians. Sometimes he was worshiped as a god.

ALWAYS A MAN?

The Egyptians believed men and women should do different jobs because they are different. They believed that being pharaoh was a man's job (so was washing the laundry in a river). A queen could rule Egypt for her son while he grew up, but she was not supposed to rule alone. Hatshepsut tried to do this.

Hatshepsut took over in 1479 B.C., when the young Thutmose III became pharaoh. She began to call herself pharaoh not queen. She dressed as a pharaoh. She made laws in her name and not his name. We do not know what happened to Hatshepsut. All descriptions about her as pharaoh were chipped off carvings or painted over. Descriptions of her as queen were left alone.

The death mask of the pharaoh Tutankhamun, who died in 1327 B.C. It took 22.5 pounds (10.23 kg) of gold sheets to cover the mask. Pharaohs were buried with many valuable things. They had to be buried with everything they would need in the **afterlife.**

Next in importance to the **pharaoh** were his governors who ran large parts of Egypt. The mayors who ran the big towns, like Memphis and Thebes, were also important. Important **officials** also had religious jobs.

SENNEFER

Sennefer ran Thebes and the royal estates nearby for the pharaoh Amenhotep II in about 1400 B.C. He was also chief priest of the temples there. His brother was chief advisor to the pharaoh. His family had worked for earlier pharaohs. The family was rich and powerful.

Sennefer had a wife, Senetnay (who looked after the pharaoh's children), and two daughters, Nofret and Tuya. As chief priest, he took part in important religious ceremonies. He had a large house in Thebes and estates nearby. He had to visit all the places he was in charge of to make sure the officials that worked for him were doing their jobs properly. They did most of the work. But it was Sennefer who would be blamed by the pharaoh if anything went wrong.

ANCIENT EGYPTIAN **SCRIBES** WROTE BOOKS ON HOW TO BEHAVE. THIS ADVICE IS FOR OFFICIALS ON HOW TO SETTLE ARGUMENTS:

If you are a man who leads, listen calmly to one who pleads. Don't stop him telling you all he has planned to say. A man in distress wants to pour out his heart more than he wants to win.

Most of what we know about Sennefer comes from his **tomb** in the Valley of the Kings near Thebes. The large pictures of people on the walls are Sennefer and Senetnay.

Ordinary **priests** did most of the day-to-day work in **temples**. The **pharaoh** and his chief priests only visited the biggest and most important temples.

Priests worked in the temple for one month out of every four. There were different kinds of jobs. Sem-priests performed the ceremonies. Lector priests read the prayers aloud. After each month in the temple, they spent three months doing their government job. They had to be trained as **scribes** for both jobs.

USERHAT

Userhat was a sem-priest in Thebes in about 1280 B.C. Sem-priests regularly took part in religious ceremonies including the burial ceremony. They wore leopard-skin cloaks. Userhat lived on the temple estates. His house was not large but had several rooms and a garden. He had a wife, Shepset, but no children. His mother probably lived with his family. When he was not working as a priest, he helped run the temple estates.

In this picture painted in about 1300 B.C., a sem-priest is performing a burial ceremony. Userhat would have performed ceremonies like this many times.

WABS

Wabs were the least important **priests**. Like all priests, they were **scribes** who worked as priests for one month out of every four. They cleaned the **temple**, killed **sacrifices**, and carried **tomb models** or even **mummies** in funeral processions.

The scribes, who are measuring the fields in the top picture and writing down the amounts of corn in the bottom, may have been wabs.

A GREEK WRITER VISITED EGYPT IN 450 B.C. HE WROTE ABOUT THEIR PRIESTS. HE DID NOT ALWAYS GET THE DETAILS RIGHT!

Priests shave their bodies all over every other day to stop getting lice. They only wear linen clothes and shoes made from the papyrus plant. They wash in cold water twice a day and twice at night. There is food that they are not allowed to eat like pigs and some fish.

— HOREMKENESI —

Horemkenesi was a wab priest in the temples at Karnak and Medinet Habu in about 1500 B.C. But he was more important as an official. He grew up in Deir-el-Medina, where the workmen who built the tombs in the Valley of the Kings lived. He trained as a scribe. By the time he died at age 50, he ran Deir-el-Medina. He made sure the workmen had enough food and tools. He paid them and organized their workdays and days off. He was also in charge of reorganizing the old tombs, which had already been broken into by tomb robbers. Old tombs were cleared, mummies rewrapped, and treasures put away. We know a lot about his work, but we do not know if he was married or had children.

The mummy case of Horemkenesi. A lot of the writing on it is religious. But it also tells us who he was and what his jobs were. The writing on the coffin explains that he was a wab priest and also the foreman at Deir.

Women could be **priestesses**, usually for a goddess not a god. There were far fewer priestesses than **priests**. Most worked in the **temples** of the goddess Hathor.

Women could not train as **scribes,** so they could not read and write. This meant they could not do any work in the temple that involved reading prayers aloud or keeping records.

MUSIC

Priestesses provided the music, singing, and dancing in all **religious ceremonies** including festivals for gods and goddesses and funerals.

Many women from important families worked as *"musicians and dancers to the temple"* at temples for important gods like Amun. Unlike priests, they had no other work. They worked for the temple all year round.

This carving of the priestess Deniu-en-Khons was found in her tomb.
She is making an offering to the god Horus.

Temples varied greatly in size. Some were small. Others were part of big **estates** with many farmers, craftsmen, and even sailors working for them. Temples were built in towns, in the countryside, and at important burial places. All the temples had **priests**, and **religious ceremonies** were carried out at the temples each day.

SERVING THE GOD

Three times a day, the priests washed in a special pool and put on clean clothes. Then they went to the temple. Ordinary people could not go into the temple. The priests went room by room to the god's **shrine**. As they approached the shrine, the rooms became smaller and darker. Wabs stayed in the outer rooms. Only the chief priest went into the shrine. He took the statue of the god out of the shrine. He washed, oiled, and dressed it before offering it food. Then he put it away. On special days, priests took the statue out of the temple and marched around the town with it. This gave ordinary people a chance to see the statue of the god and a religious ceremony.

A large temple estate like this one had a royal palace,
workshops, and farming land, as well as a temple.

THE AFTERLIFE

The Ancient Egyptians believed that the dead came back to life. This meant that people had to be buried properly with all of the things they would need in the **afterlife**.

MUMMIES

It was important to keep dead bodies in the best state possible, ready for their owner's afterlife. During the Ancient Egyptian period, people tried more and more complicated ways of preserving bodies. Most of the time, they **embalmed** them (made them into **mummies**). This means they took out all the soft parts that would rot (the brain, heart, lungs, and liver). They soaked the body in salt to draw out the liquids that made the body rot. Then they wrapped the body in bandages soaked in oil.

Poor people could not afford to embalm their dead. They buried them in the hot **desert** sand. This preserved bodies just as well—better than some embalming did! Some still exist today.

Embalmers mostly worked outside in tents that were open on two sides. This let the wind blow through and take the odors away.

EVIDENCE FROM THE TIME

Some **tomb paintings** show **mummies** being made. People at the time wrote about how mummies were made too.

A painting from a coffin made in about 600 B.C. It shows the stages of making a mummy. The black figure is the mummy.

A GREEK WRITER VISITED EGYPT IN 450 B.C. HE SAW HOW THE ANCIENT EGYPTIANS MADE MUMMIES:

They take out the brains through the nose with a hook. They cut open the side of the body and take out the parts there. Then they clean out the space and stitch up the body. They cover it for 70 days in salt. Then they wash it and wrap it from head to toe in cloth strips.

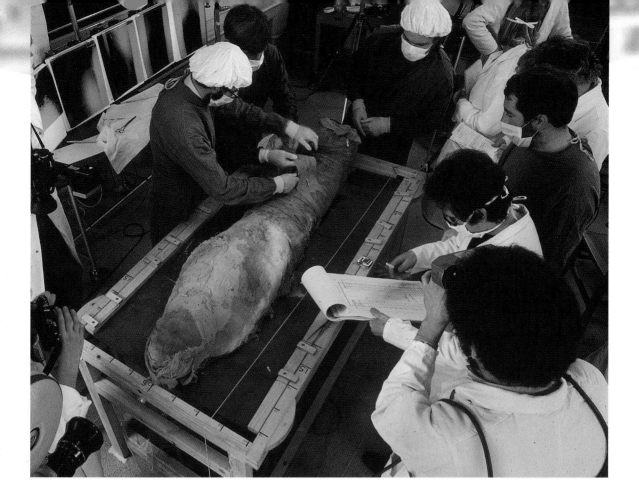

NEW EVIDENCE

Many mummies have survived from Ancient Egypt. **Archaeologists** can study them. They use x-rays to photograph what is inside the bandages. They have even unwrapped mummies. Then they can study the body and the bandages.

Archaeologists unwrapping one mummy saw she had been unwrapped before by Ancient Egyptians! The Egyptians had found that her legs were broken. They made new legs from clay and reeds. It shows they believed she had to walk in the **afterlife**.

Unwrapping Horemkensi's mummy (see page 15). The table was built with moving parts so it could be moved during unwrapping instead of moving the mummy.

When a body had been **embalmed**, the **priests** took over. They took the body to the burial place, often across the river from the town. Burial places had to be close so relatives could visit the chapels of the **tombs** with gifts of food and drink.

BURIAL PLACES

Burial places were usually in the **desert**. Servants filled the tomb with furniture, food, and other things the tomb owner would need in the **afterlife**—even mummified pets! While this was going on, the priests held the **religious ceremonies** that would make sure the tomb owner's spirit could move in and out of the body when it needed to. When they had finished, the tomb was sealed up.

PEOPLE VISITING THE DEAD LEFT MESSAGES AS WELL AS FOOD. THESE MESSAGES COULD BE MEAN:

How are you? Look, I am your beloved on earth so speak up for me! I gave you a proper funeral so drive off the illness in my limbs! Send me a dream to show you are fighting for me there.

Priests performing a religious
ceremony called "the opening of
the mouth" in the burial place.
The chapel is behind the mummy.

Egypt was very cut off from the rest of the world. The **desert** separated Egypt from Sinai and Libya. A break in the level of the Nile River made huge waterfalls, so ships could not cross into Nubia. The Delta marshes helped to cut Egypt off from the Mediterranean. Egypt did trade and fight with other countries from time to time. It was the **pharaoh** who made those decisions.

TRADE

The Ancient Egyptians grew everything they needed, so they did not need to trade regularly with another country. But sometimes the harvest failed and they needed to buy grain from other countries.

WAR

All pharaohs had an army. Mostly they did not want to take over other countries. They just wanted to keep Egypt safe. Most ordinary soldiers had to join the army. They fought on foot, using spears and bows and arrows. After horses were brought into Egypt (in about 1600 B.C.) important soldiers fought in horse-drawn chariots.

This is an Egyptian **tomb model** of soldiers on the march. These soldiers were found in the tomb of Mesehti, a local governor who would have commanded an army in real life.

EVIDENCE FROM THE TIME

How do we know how Egypt was organized? How do we know what **priests** did, what **officials** did, and that people did both jobs at once? We know by reading the records from the time and the writing on **tomb** walls and **mummy** cases. Written information was vital to the running of Ancient Egypt. Only **scribes** could write, so only scribes could be officials and priests.

NEW EVIDENCE

Each time **archaeologists** unwrap a mummy or read the writing on a mummy case, they find out more about people from the time.

Historians once thought that a high priest had to be an important official too, like Sennefer. Now we know this is not true. Archaeologists who studied Horemkensi found out that he was an important official but one of the least important kinds of priests.

Writing left by scribes tells us a lot about life in Ancient Egypt. We can even figure out that a school for scribes would have looked like this.

GLOSSARY

afterlife Egyptians believed the dead come back to life. The afterlife was their life after death, which lasted forever in a place called The Field of Reeds.

amulets small magic symbols worn to keep a person safe

archaeologists people who dig up and study things left behind from past times

crops plants that farmers grow for food or to use in other ways (to make clothes, baskets, or paper)

desert a dry place that has little or no rain all year

embalming a way of keeping a body from rotting, usually by drying it out and wrapping it in strips of oiled cloth

estate a large piece of land with homes and farmland all run by the same person

mummies bodies of dead people that have been preserved

officials people chosen to work for the **pharaoh** who could tell others what to do

pharaoh the king who ruled Egypt

priest a person who worked in a temple serving a god or goddess

priestess a female priest

religious ceremonies special times when people go to one place to pray to a god or goddess

sacrifice something given to a god or goddess as a gift. If the sacrifice was a living thing, it was killed before it was given. Food and items such as jewels could be given as a sacrifice too.

scribes the only people in Ancient Egypt who could read and write. Scribes ran the country for the **pharaoh.**

shrine a place where a statue of a god or goddess is kept so that people can pray to it

temple a place where gods and goddesses are worshiped

tomb a place where someone is buried

tomb models tiny carvings or pottery shapes of people and things that were put in **tombs**

tomb paintings paintings on the walls of **tombs**

INDEX

archaeology   23, 28

clothes   5, 7, 11, 13, 14, 17, 21, 22, 25, 27, 29

doctors   6

education   11, 12, 29

embalming   20, 21

estates   10, 12, 18

families   10, 12, 24

food   14, 15, 24, 26

mummies   14, 15, 20–3

officials   5, 10, 11, 15, 28

pharaohs   4, 5, 8, 10, 12, 26
   Hatshepsut   8
   Narmer   4
   Rameses II   5
   Tutankhamun   9

religion   10, 13
   afterlife   7, 13, 20, 23, 24
   amulets   6

religion (continued)
   ceremonies   10, 12, 13, 16, 18, 24
   funerals   13, 14, 16, 24
   gods   6–8, 18
   goddesses   6, 16
   magic   6
   priests   5, 10, 12–4, 18, 28
   priestesses   16, 17
   temples   5, 10, 12, 16, 18–9

scribes   11–4, 16, 28, 29

tombs   11, 15, 24
   tomb models   14, 24, 27
   tomb paintings   11, 13, 14, 22, 28

trade   26

war   5, 26

writing   7, 14, 28

MORE BOOKS TO READ

Clayton, Peter A. *The Valley of the Kings.* Chatham, NJ: Raintree Steck-Vaughn. 1995.

Green, Robert. *Tutankhamun.* Danbury, CT: Franklin Watts Incorporated. 1996.

Shuter, Jane. *The Ancient Egyptians.* Des Plaines, IL: Heinemann Library. 1997.